Live in The Little

52 Ways To Find The Extra In The Ordinary

Monica Scalf

ISBN:978-1-451-53199-2

To Brian, thank you for making all of life's little moments even better.
&
To Mom, thank you for teaching me to live LARGE in the little.

INTRODUCTION

I'm sure that you have a thousand things on your TO DO list. In fact, they're probably running like a ticker tape through your head right now. It seems as if we're all overbooked, overwhelmed, and stressed out. A few years ago that's exactly where I found myself. While being a part time professor, a full time mom, and a constant stress-a-holic, I realized that I had let too much joy drain from my life. I was doing all of the things that I **had** to do, but none of the things that truly inspired me and increased the joy, energy, and humor in my life. Sound familiar? I think we've all been there a time or two.

As I looked around, I noticed that I wasn't the only one in hurry up mode, constantly *just getting through the day.* Friends, family and colleagues had coated themselves in the responsibilites of the daily grind too. After some much needed reflection time, I figured that there had to be a way to both meet the demands of daily living *and* create joy and meaning while doing it. I wanted to figure out how to make the ordinary *extraordinary.*

I made a conscious effort to find more joy in the everyday. Along my journey I began a blog called *The Ordinary Matters* where I've shared what I've learned about capturing daily happiness. Now, I'm sharing a collection of those weekly *pick me ups* in a book. On the days when it doesn't feel like there's any extra in your ordinary, I hope this book reminds you that there is.

*"Sometimes your joy is the source of your smile, but sometimes
your smile can be the source of your Joy."*
Thich Nhat Hanh

CHAPTER 1

FILL YOUR JOY WELL

Ok, we've all heard this simple piece of wisdom, *Take Time to Fill Up Your Well*, but it's about as easy as, oh let's say, understanding the current tax code or passing a bar exam. And further more, it ranks right up there with bungee jumping and lion taming on the scary chart too!

The reason it's so difficult is because we've trained ourselves to use the distractions of everyday life as the perfect excuse to never fill up our own wells. It's scary because when we finally get a chance to do it, we've forgotten what will fill us up. Not knowing what brings us joy makes us feel like we've lost our way.

The great thing is once we start paying attention, it's pretty easy to get back on the path. Sometimes we think that joy needs to be reserved for special occasions or big life events, or that the only thing that makes us happy is more stuff. I'm challenging you to figure out when you experience joy in the routine of things.

Pick one day this week, and every time you experience

joy, stop and think about how your body feels. I experience joy when I watch David Letterman at night, hear a song that I can't help but dance to, and listen to my nine year old singing at the top of his lungs. Joy for me is like a smile that radiates both inward and outward. It just feels good in my body. If you're having trouble, think of a joyous moment in your life, close your eyes, picture it vividly and then push the SAVE button in your mind to remember what your body felt like in that moment.

Sometimes, it's easier to focus on the struggle of the day than on the joy. We get used to downloading everything that went wrong for the day to whomever will listen. Figure out a way to give more attention to the joy filled moments. Once we start paying attention our bodies will naturally seek out more of these moments. We'll get in a groove, and before we know it our joy wells will be running over.

Little Idea

Make a map of your Joy Buzzers. Put the word Joy Buzzers in the middle of a blank piece of paper. Now fill the surrounding area with all of the things that really make your heart beat faster because you enjoy them so much: people, songs, movies, books, activites, etc. Post it somewhere so you will see it everyday this week. How can you incorporate more of these things into your daily routine?

"Take a music bath once or twice a week for a few seasons.
You'll find it is to the soul what a water bath is to a body."
Oliver Wendell Holmes

CHAPTER 2

TINA TURNER THERAPY

Admit it. You blast the radio and sing out loud when no one else is in the car. You have that one song you know every word to, and you've even made up hand motions to go along. Ok, maybe you haven't gone that far, but there's no denying that a good song makes all of us want to move; it gets us energized; and it can change our attitude in 3 minutes or less.

Do you remember the television show Ally McBeal (skinny lawyer girl, early nineties)? Ally always had a soundtrack in her head. She had a "theme song" that would pump her up and get her through the day. This week your job is to find that song. It may take some research, but time invested in YOU always pays back tenfold.

Once you find your song (or you may already know what it is) then your job is to listen to it throughout the week. Be aware of how your mood changes after you listen to it. Think about ways you can use music to your advantage in other areas of your life. Begin collecting songs that make you feel good. If nothing else, let the exercise remind you that you have your own personal likes and dislikes, separate from your spouse and the rest of your family. Relish in the fact that it is "your song" (or songs) chosen by you!

Little Idea

Make your own personal playlist to have as daily inspiration when you need it. Here are a dozen to get you moving.

"Proud Mary" Tina Turner
"Thankful" Kelly Clarkson
"Gonna Breakthrough" Mary J. Blige
"Golden" Jill Scott
"Sisters Are Doin' It for Themselves" Annie Lennox
"Settlin" Sugarland
"Uptight (Everything's Alright)" Stevie Wonder
"Put on a Happy Face" Tony Bennett
"Start Me Up" The Rolling Stones
"That's Why God Made Mexico" Tim McGraw
"Put Your Records On" Corinne Bailey Rae
"Everything's Coming Up Roses" Rosemary Clooney

"To be really great in little things, to be truly noble and heroic in the insipid details of everyday life, is a virtue so rare as to be worthy of canonization." - Harriet Beecher Stowe

CHAPTER 3

THE MARVELOUS MUNDANE

Let me guess. You hardly have a minute to spend on yourself; when you finally get to sit down you're crazy tired; and the thought of adding one more thing to your day is about as appealing as trying on swimwear under fluorescent lights. I know I've been there, and some days I think I'll be there forever. The toughest time to remember how miraculous life can be is in the midst of the daily drudgery.

What I'm proposing may sound a bit absurd, especially if you're reading this after a long day. If so, go to sleep, wake up, have a cup of coffee and come back in the morning. Ok, you're either still with me or you're back (Good Morning!), so here's my big suggestion:

Be the miracle worker in your house for the next week beginning today.

I know, you're saying, "I already am!" Aren't we all? I'm challenging you to be an even bigger and better miracle worker by injecting little miracles into the lives of those around you on a daily basis for the next week.

Why you ask? Because by showing others around you how much you care, you'll get your own personal side benefit – ENERGY! The reason this works is because when we do little things like this it causes us to be engaged in life. We get out of the hum-drum and into the here and now. It's the same reason that people love vacations and holidays – these events allow for a diversion from the monotonous tasks of daily life.

When we learn how to create our own fun diversions in the context of day to day living, we've achieved a view from which there is no turning back! You'll get addicted to how much energy you get from creating a playful life in the realm of real life.

Little Idea
Make someone's day with one of these simple acts.

- *Leave a sweet treat in your loved one's car.*
- *Write a note and mail it to your sweetie at home or (even better) at work.*
- *Write a favorite quote on a post-it note and put it up on the bathroom mirror to share.*
- *Call and leave a voicemail for a friend telling them how thankful you are for them.*
- *Compliment someone in front of others.*

"In a minute there is time."
T.S. Eliot

CHAPTER 4

THE 60 SECOND RITUAL

Time is tight, right? There's a new four letter word in our vocabulary . . . B-U-S-Y. I'm sure you're extremely busy most of the time. So am I. But, I've got a secret that helps me escape each day. Actually, T.S. Eliot gets the credit for it. It's a line from his famous poem "The Love Song of J. Alfred Prufrock".

In a minute there is time.

Sorry to go all English teacher on you, but I think he was on to something. *In a minute there is time.* Time to do what, you ask? Aha, I have an answer: Time to do a ritual in 60 seconds (or less, for you overachievers).

What can you do each day that takes less than a minute yet makes time slow down for you? Here's an easy one that I do most days. But first, let me give you some back story. (I know, hurry up, you're BUSY! I'll make it quick.)

Several years ago, I stayed at a hotel where they turned the bed down each night while we were away at dinner. Along with fluffing the pillows and rolling back the covers, they dimmed the lamps that were on each bedside table. They also placed a soothing saying on the pillow dubbing it a Reflection Card. Sounds kind of corny, but after a few days of this, I got used to arriving back to our prepped room. I noticed that each lamp had a plug-in dimmer switch that sat atop the bedside tables. This little gadget allowed a regular lamp to be dim or bright by moving the easy sliding switch. So, the first week I got home, when I was battling vacation withdrawal, I went in search of the same dimmer switch for my own nightstand. My local big box hardware store had one, and for approximately $15, I had a piece of my vacation in my everyday life.

Each night, sometime in the early evening, I try to pass through my bedroom to turn off the other lights and turn on and dim the lamp on my side of the bed. It takes about oh, 4 seconds. For such a small change, the payoff (for me) is huge. It's relaxing to come to bed, and in a small way, feel like I've done something for myself for the day.

You may have other rituals you do already. If so, appreciate the place they have in your life. If not, this week try to think of at least one quick thing you could do daily that will signal your effort to take care of yourself amidst the busyness of life.

Little Idea
Buy a dimmer switch and watch it brighten your life.

"Every small positive change we make in ourselves repays us in confidence in the future."
Alice Walker

CHAPTER 5

SMILE

I'm a sucker for a good acronym – you know a word that stands for a longer phrase – so I couldn't go much longer without introducing one. Ready? Wait for it . . .

SMILE = Saving My Interesting Life Everyday.

What have you done lately to save YOUR interesting life? I'm guessing that you could probably tick off a dozen or so things you've done to help others enhance their lives recently. Can you say the same for yourself? If so, hooray! If not, then this is a great opportunity to take a day or two this week to do something interesting in your own eyes.

This can be as simple as buying a different brand of toothpaste (ok, that's for real beginners) or as adventurous as planning that European excursion you've been waiting your whole life to take.

The goal here is to be aware that you can make choices for yourself every day to shake things up a bit: make a new recipe, wear a color you never wear, treat yourself to a white mocha latte. You get the idea. Only you can decide what works for you. I get stuck in a rut from time to time, and it's only when I remind myself that life is supposed to be fun for me too that I begin to see ways to incorporate a little more SMILE into my day.

I'm guessing there was a time that we can all remember, maybe those college days, when we felt the exhilaration of making big and little decisions that kept our lives moving forward. When we look for opportunities big and small to make our lives more interesting, we can have this same feeling again. Don't be surprised if your attitude is contagious!

Little Idea

Need some SMILE inspiration? Look no further.

Reach out to someone you've lost touch with.
Take a new workout class. Ever tried Zumba?
Rearrange the furniture.
Investigate classes you can take online.
Buy a travel guide for that dream vacation.
Be the person who introduces herself to someone new.
Join a community club or bookclub.
Plan a dinner party with 6 new guests.
Make a new recipe with someone's help.
Write a fan letter to a favorite author, actor, or leader.

"The human race has only one really effective weapon
and that is laughter."
Mark Twain

CHAPTER 6

EASY QUIZ

To follow is the world's easiest question.

Do you want or need to do any of the following?
- reduce your stress
- lower your blood pressure
- elevate your mood
- boost your immune system
- improve your brain functioning
- protect your heart
- connect more with others
- foster instant relaxation
- feel good

Hold on a minute, I think I just heard a resounding, "YES". Oh, that was me talking to myself. If you're emphatically nodding too, this task is just for you, and it's super easy. All you need to do is . . . LAUGH MORE.

Funny, giggle, ha-ha, hee-hee, that's all there is to it.

Find something funny to watch, read, look at or appreciate, and your body will thank you for it. And coming from a person who can mangle the punch line of the easiest of jokes, fear not, you don't have to BE funny to appreciate humor. You just have to be tuned in to the humor that's all around you, and be willing to laugh.

Laughter increases creativity, productivity, and communication. I'm betting that we could all use more of these qualities in our daily lives. One of the easiest ways to get a little more laughter into your life is to spend some time with girlfriends. Women have an amazing ability to get together and LAUGH. Some of my biggest belly laughs have been in the company of girlfriends who are sharing the humorous side of everyday life. One gut busting belly laugh can do amazing things for your body and your attitude. So get laughing!

Little Idea

*Take a "Comedy Break" most days this week. Spend five minutes doing something that will make you laugh. If you have more time, watch **Here and Now**, Ellen DeGeneres' HBO comedy special on DVD. I laughed out loud until my stomach hurt.*

"Life is a great bundle of little things."
Oliver Wendell Holmes

CHAPTER 7

SMALL CHANGE, BIG PAYOFF

Several weeks ago, I had to get a filling replaced with a permanent crown. This particular filling had been hanging around since the early 80's when silver fillings, among other things (like Jarts), were still safe. After 20 years of Swedish Fish and Bit O Honey, I guess the filling was ready to retire, and one day it just cracked.

I never willingly go sit in a chair where mere inches away they house needles that require the words, "You may want to close your eyes," but I visited the dentist, endured, and emerged with virtually a new tooth and the satisfaction that I had fixed a problem.

Two weeks post crown seating (that's dental lingo), the tooth was still painful and the left side of my mouth hadn't seen food in weeks. Previous dental experience, of which there is much, told me that I needed another appointment. Bracing myself for the worst . . . I entered the dentist's office with sweaty palms and a rapid heartbeat.

First, the dentist had me bite down. Ouch. Pain! Next, she had me open. She got out the drill that makes the noise we

all know by heart. My feet tensed. This was going to hurt. Whirr
. . . Whirr. A mere 5 seconds later . . . "Ok, bite down again."
I bit gingerly. Nothing. I bit again a little harder. Nothing. No
Pain. "It's great," I said, half amazed. "Good, all done," she said.
"Sometimes just a minor adjustment on the crown can make all
the difference," she said.

The only good thing about pain is that it reminds you
how nice life is without it. I spent the rest of the day enjoying the
lack of pain in my mouth and thinking about how something so
small (and painless) could make such a big difference.

I started thinking of other small adjustments that needed
to be made in my life. I decided not to make them all at once,
but rather to choose one, do it, and feel the satisfaction that came
with doing it. What I did doesn't matter. It's too mundane to even
mention, but I can guarantee I'll make another small adjustment
soon. The energy burst is worth it. Sometimes we overlook the
benefit of making small corrections along the way. Or, we think
there is so much to be done that doing something small won't
matter, so we choose to do nothing. I've learned differently.

Little Idea
*Make a quick list of the small adjustments you can make in your
life this week that will make a big difference.*

"Nothing great was ever achieved without enthusiasm."
Ralph Waldo Emerson

CHAPTER 8

MAKE THE CHOICE

Everybody loves getting a gift, right? Any kid (and some adults) can tell you that the anticipation of opening a nicely wrapped package is half the fun. The other half of the fun belongs to the giver of the gift.

You can be a constant gift giver by giving away something that is free, good for you, and accessible to anyone, anywhere, anytime:

Enthusiasm

I'm not talking about the fake enthusiasm that exudes from the fitting room attendant that tells the shopper a door down from you that the pastel pink pleated pant suit "looks fabulous" and " is absolutely still in style." I'm talking about a genuine feeling emitted by particular people on a regular basis in the midst of day-to-day life. You can probably think of someone who brings energy, levity, and fun to most any situation. They keep life interesting, and others love to be around them. I used to think that these people had a natural gift. But experience has taught me otherwise; *Enthusiasm is a choice.*

People who have an enthusiastic attitude on a regular basis have made a conscious choice to view life in a positive way. They make it look so easy that we tend to forget that effort is a part of enthusiasm.

Some situations are easy to be enthusiastic about, but it's the smaller stuff of life that can be most affected by enthusiasm. Making an effort to inject enthusiasm into the routine of things can change your perception of your daily life. You don't have to overdo it: cleaning out the trash can with fervent enthusiasm may cause your family undue concern. But, you can start with just one thing - like being enthusiastic when hearing of a friend's accomplishment, or being enthusiastic when you first see your children after school, or being the one who brings the enthusiasm to a difficult task you are doing with others.

I've been given the gift of enthusiasm many times by family, friends, co-workers, students, and even strangers. Each time I receive it, I feel better mentally and physically. The enthusiasm of others allows me to conquer what I think is impossible and turns routine experiences into something memorable.

Little Idea
Put enthusiasm to work for you (and others) by consciously choosing one task that you will be enthusiastic about.

"I've always thought best when I wrote."
Toni Morrison

CHAPTER 9

THE 10 MINUTE PROBLEM SOLVER

This idea is a great way to get unstuck. From projects as simple as cleaning out a closet to decisions as complicated as changing careers, all of us find ourselves unable to move forward at times. If you have the courage to try this idea, it may help you see your sticking point in a new way.

The technique is called freewriting. And to complete it you need only three simple things:

- ten minutes
- an issue you are stuck on
- and a way to write

There are two simple rules:

- You have to write for ten solid minutes with as little stopping time as possible.
- You aren't allowed to edit yourself in the process.

In other words, keep the pen or the typing fingers moving as quickly as you can -- that way you'll be less likely to break rule #2.

Here's an example:

*I'm just trying to figure out why I've been stuck when it comes to
_____. I don't know what to write. I've never done
this before. I think I'm stuck because _____. I
wonder if I really want to _____. This exercise
seems really stupid, but I'm going to write for 8 more minutes.
(and on, and on)*

You can insert obscenities and sarcastic remarks where
necessary. I promise no one will read them, and I'll never know.
You don't have to share your writing with anyone else or even
save it for yourself. Hopefully, at the end of ten minutes you've
emptied your brain of all the things that were keeping you stuck,
and you've come up with your own next step. The writing is just
a way to get you back in the flow of knowing what the next step
should be.

This technique seems so simple that you can't imagine
how filling a page will help you improve your daily life, but if
you give it a chance, I know it will. It has often worked for me
and others that I know. It just may help you put the Extra in your
Ordinary!

Little Idea
*Use the freewriting technique at least once. It works for various
segments of your daily life (work, home, parenting, relationships),
and it's only a ten-minute investment.*

"Winners have the ability to step back from the canvas of their lives like an artist gaining perspective. They make their lives a work of art - an individual masterpiece."

Denis Waitley

CHAPTER 10

PROPER PERSPECTIVE PLEASE

There's an old joke that goes:

What do you get when you play a country song backwards?

Answer: You get your car back, your wife back, your dog back, your house back . . . insert laughter. You get the picture. I'm sure you've heard it before.

Ok, mine's not nearly as funny, but here it goes:

Q: What do you get when you play a country song forward?

A: Perspective.

The other night after a weekend of running kids around, trying to do last minute laundry, and surveying the general disarray of my house and my life, I felt worn out, overwhelmed and stressed. I was slipping into poor me as I schlepped a load of laundry into my bedroom, clicked on the television, and began folding. I caught Trace Adkins singing his song "You're Gonna Miss This" on the Academy of Country Music Awards. As I listened to the lyrics, I began to realize how small I was being.

You're gonna miss this

You're gonna want this back

You're gonna wish these days hadn't gone by so fast
These are some good times
So take a good look around
You may not know it now
But you're gonna miss this

In less than a few minutes, I began to see things in proper perspective. I had so much to be grateful for, and I was wasting my time feeling pitiful.

The word perspective comes from the Latin word perspicere meaning to look through, to see clearly. In that moment, I was able to see clearly how much I had to be grateful for. Perspective is being able to tune into the truth and see a situation in its proper context instead of staying stuck on a station that replays our misperceptions about how tough life is.

Merely being aware enough to step back and ask yourself if there is another way to look at and see a situation clearly helps us to keep a healthy perspective about the demands of daily life.

Little Idea

Great songs, great movies, and great books all have the power to pull us out of our own small worlds to see ourselves in a different way. Take the time to enjoy something that makes you feel part of a bigger world.

"Life will always be to a large extent what we ourselves make it."
Samuel Smiles

Chapter 11

The Stuff of Life

George Carlin, comic extraordinaire, once claimed that the meaning of life revolves around, "trying to find a place for your stuff." His hilarious rant on society's collective fascination with thinking about, keeping, and transporting our "stuff" is a great reminder of the odd (and funny) relationship we have with our things.

I realize I too have some quirks when it comes to my stuff. For instance, when I get ready for vacation, I give weeks of attention to what I'll be taking with me - piling up and saving clothes, collecting just the right sunscreens, and even purchasing the travel size of everything, including specific snacks (Can anyone say Dark Chocolate Peanut M&M's?) for the ride! I usually forget a thing or two, but for the most part I'm well prepared and ready to enjoy my holiday from life. The time I put into figuring out what to carry with me pays off in comfort during the journey.

Recently, I've decided to transfer this same philosophy to my daily life. You see, before I would haphazardly grab what I thought I needed for the day as I dashed out of the house. I would later find myself wishing for a variety of things I didn't think to bring with me – a magazine for the wait, a bottle of water to wash down an Advil, and even sometimes just a pen!

I'm sure some of you are always properly prepared, but for those of you like me I'm suggesting investing a few minutes each day to gather the right stuff before leaving the house. What things could you easily carry with you that could potentially offer you a little piece of comfort during the day? A diet Coke, a pad of paper, a book you might get a chance to start – the possibilities are endless. Using our own stuff to create a better daily experience doesn't cost anything. The only thing we have to pay is attention.

Little Idea
Need some grab 'n go inspiration?

- *Put grapes in baggies and freeze to grab a healthy snack on your way out the door.*
- *A book of essays like **Naked** by David Sedaris makes waiting in the carpool line funnier.*
- *Keep a small pencil bag in your purse filled with sharpened pencils and a few pens along with a mini notebook.*
- *An ipod is the perfect prescription for instant calm during a stressful day.*

"He is the happiest, be he king or peasant, who finds peace in his home."

Johann Wolfgang von Goethe

CHAPTER 12

THE ART OF REINVENTION

Recently I was walking around my house dreaming of all the things I wanted to change about the space. As I walked through my dining room, I envisioned a new chandelier. I turned the corner into my kitchen and pictured built in window seats with extra storage and extra pillows -- the perfect place to curl up on a rainy day. Tripping over a random football, of which there are many sizes and colors around my house, brought me back to reality.

In that instant, I realized that many of my re-modeling projects would only ever be completed in my mind. Seems like other more pressing, but less exciting, things jump to the head of the To Purchase list - like dental work and braces. (Although I'm not complaining, sometime I'll tell you about my love / hate relationships with dentists. I've spent my fair share of "new sofa" money on root canals and crowns!)

Knowing that I didn't have the luxury of a total remodel, I thought of a suitable and much cheaper alternative – reinvention. Since the outdoor season was upon us, I decided to begin in our much ignored screened in porch. A gallon of sky blue paint, an investment of a few hours, and a husband willing to hang a porch swing later, our re-invented room was complete. The mini project has brought a new energy to our house. Everyone in the family naturally congregates to the newly prepped space. I love it (even more than a new chandelier)!

I'm envisioning some other reinventions happening soon. Using what we already have and re-purposing some things from around the house will shake things up a bit, and create some great energy. If Madonna can reinvent herself multiple times, it should be fairly stress free to do some of our own domestic reinvention. And you don't even have to be a Material Girl!

Little Idea

Try noticing how the things around your home are placed. Have those silk flower arrangements been in the same place since you moved in? Pick a dozen things (little or big) to move around. You'll be surprised by how these little changes can give you a whole new perspective or appreciation for items you've had forever.

"All you need to write a letter is a pen, a piece of paper, and you.
Get into the envelope and seal the flap!"
Wilfred Peterson

CHAPTER 13

WAIT A MINUTE, MR. POSTMAN

Who among us didn't have a shoebox full of skillfully folded notes that were passed in the halls of high school? Remember how we painstakingly drew our bubble-lettered signatures and perfected our smiley faces?

I finally let go of most of my high school notes in the years after college, but I did keep a few. Every so often I run across them while de-cluttering, and they always make me laugh. It's so fun to have a mini piece of history (even if a bit of melodrama is involved) right in my hands!

With the invention of e-mail, texting, i-chatting and more, the written note may be on the endangered species list. That's why I thought this tip from a reader was such a great one. She writes:

Here's something else I try to do. Write a note a week to someone--not e-mail... For some reason, it makes you feel good!

When this tip came in, I went to my local Michael's Arts and Crafts store and armed myself with a box of fun and funky assorted textured cards. A good pen and a sheet of stamps kept right by my desk. I was all set to try my card a week.

I haven't accomplished my mission every week, but I have written more notes by hand in the last few months. And I have to agree, it just makes me feel good! Imagine the surprise your husband, parent, child, friend, or even former high school teacher would feel if you took the time to write them a note. I think they'd feel pretty Extraordinary and so would you!

Little Idea

Keep handwritten letters off of the endangered species list. Set up your own letter writing station. Get a decorative box, fill it with some of your favorite papers and cards, a nice pen, postage stamps, envelope seals, return address labels, etc. Then see how easy it is to send a note to someone when the occassion arises. Make a goal of at least one a month. You're guaranteed to brighten someone's day.

"The happiest people are those who think the most interesting thoughts. They are the cause of happiness in others."
William Lyon Phelps

CHAPTER 14

SEEING IS BELIEVING

Quick quiz: Look up right now and notice what's in your field of vision. If you're lucky, it's the ocean and the beach as you check your e-mail from your vacation rental. For the rest of us, it's probably something a little more mundane: pictures on our office wall, a television set beyond our laptop, or a messy cluttered desk (that's what I see!).

Next question: Can you scan the room for something that makes you feel joyful? Is there something in your field of vision that can allow you to look past the clutter and feel good? Despite my messy desk, I can look at several pictures on my bulletin board and my wall that make me feel good, that carry positive emotion, and that literally make me forget how crowded my desk has gotten.

If you don't have a photo or piece of art nearby that brings you joy, maybe you should consider introducing one into your space. Why? Because according to brain scientists, vision trumps all senses. Your brain uses over half of its resources to consume what's in your visual field. And what we see determines our perception of our reality.

Consider this example. A group of brain researchers in Europe studying the effects of vision on perception wondered what would happen if they dropped odorless and tasteless red dye into white wines being tested by wine professionals. Pretty tricky, huh? Would the testers use red wine or white wine vocabulary when describing the wine? Would both their taste buds and their well-trained noses be fooled by the sight of the wine?

You guessed it. Every one of the tasters used "red wine words" when doing their evaluation. The visual cue of the red wine was too much for the other senses to overcome. For them, seeing was believing!

For us, having a few visual cues around our homes that make us FEEL great can go a long way when we're in the midst of our daily routines. Just think of how powerful visual cues were for the embarrassed wine professionals! Look around your house or workspace for ways to use the power of vision to your advantage.

Little Idea
Make your own Joy Visual. Find a picture of a person, place or thing that holds positive emotion for you. Frame it and put it in your daily field of vision. You'll be amazed at how motivating it can be on those days that seem extra tough.

*"So as long as a person is capable of self-renewal,
they are a living being."*
Henri Frederic Amiel

CHAPTER 15

THE RESET BUTTON

Lately it seems as if I'm the gadget guru around my house. From game systems and PCs to iPods and DVRs, at times they all get a little wacky and won't work. Acting as my kids' own personal Geek Squad, I'm called to the rescue. (This usually happens when I'm right in the middle of something else. Typical, right?)

Luckily, I've discovered that almost every gadget has a RESET button or operation, and it's the first thing I try whenever there's a glitch. Nine times out of ten it works. (Let's just say every once in a while I have to stifle a variety of bad but extremely satisfying words.)

After completing another successful resuscitation of an iPod recently, I thought about how wonderful it would be if we all had our own personal RESET buttons for when we just can't get into our groove on a particular day. Whether we're feeling overwhelmed or a little blue, we all have those times when we need a system reset.

After giving it some thought, I realized it's up to us to figure out our own "reset operations" to help us feel better on one of those days. Here are some that work for me. Hopefully, they might work for you too:

• Walk - anywhere, inside or out. Even 5 minutes will get your brain moving along with your body.
• Listen - to an audio book that is uplifting and positive. Even a portion will help you to keep life in perspective.
• Throw stuff away - Some of my best self-therapy sessions have been taking 5 minutes with a trash bag and filling it up with stuff needing to be pitched.
• Put on some great music - This is the easiest way out of a slump. You can't help but move to a good song.
• UNO, anyone? - Find a child and play a game. Nothing gets you in the moment like spending time with someone whose age is still in the single digits.

Whatever you do, don't stay stuck! Figure out what helps you come back to life. I'm sure you have some great RESETs already.

Little Idea
Ask the important people in your life what they do to Reset when they're having a crummy day. You'll probably find some very practical and very successful ideas that you can incorporate into your life.

"Gratitude has the potential to change everything
from its ordinary state to being a gift."
Barbara Fredrickson

CHAPTER 16

STELLAR PERFORMANCE

If you've ever seen the stars in the Colorado sky, you know the view is pretty spectacular. Last week while spending some time relaxing in the mountains, my daughter and I were looking up at the night sky. She turned to me and said, "I never get to see stars at home." I agreed. Then this thought popped into my head:

I haven't been looking up enough.

And while the Midwest doesn't offer quite the same stellar show as the dark Western sky, I realized that getting caught up in my day to day routine sometimes makes me forget the scenic show going on in my own backyard. I know that stars make regular appearances in Ohio; I've just failed to take notice.

Focusing on a fresh view of all of the amazing people, places and things that we're surrounded by everyday can help us remove the layer of familiarity that keeps us from noticing the great things that are already a part of our daily lives.

A recent study showed that people who were consciously grateful reported the following:

Felt better about their lives
Were more optimistic
Were more energetic
Were more enthusiastic
Were more determined
Were more interested
Were more joyful
Exercised more
Had fewer illnesses
Got more sleep
Were more likely to have helped someone else

So, what can you "look up" and notice and be grateful for in a new way?

Little Idea
Nothing helps me get a fresh perspective more than making a Gratitude List. See if you can get to 100 things to be grateful for in less than 10 minutes!

"Life is trying things to see if they work."
Ray Bradbury

CHAPTER 17

NICE PROMOTION

No matter what your official or unofficial job title, you can add another to your list: Chief Creative Officer (of your own life)!

Many years ago, I walked into a bookstore and was immediately drawn to a square magnet that stated in bold black letters on a white background:

LIFE ISN'T ABOUT FINDING YOURSELF.
LIFE IS ABOUT CREATING YOURSELF.

Of course, I bought the magnet, but more than that I bought into the philosophy that the words promoted. I realized that I'm my own best chance to create the life I've always wanted – filled with joy, energy, and lots of humor! I'd say that was a pretty good buy for $4.95.

Getting creative with everyday life is easier than it sounds – especially when you realize you're the one responsible for your own FUN. And the great thing is that once you start shaking up your environment and refining your routines, others around you will want to do the same. Something as simple as buying some new and interesting things at the grocery store or as adventurous as planning a solo trip for you and your other half, signals that you're actively engaged in making life interesting. Once you start putting out your radar for ways to make life creative, the ideas will pop up all around you.

So be the leader, step up and take your promotion. Good luck, CCO!

Little Idea

Recently I posted a big piece of paper on our refrigerator that said "Scalf Family Outing. Meet here on Saturday at 12:30." The excitement in the house was palpable and the energy changed from hum-drum to anticipation. On that Saturday, we simply went to play some family volleyball, but the whole family loved the outing and the mystery of it. Several weeks later my husband posted a similar note on the fridge . . . this time, putt-putt. These were small gestures and simple outings, but the payoff in family time was huge.

"Movement is a medicine for creating change in a person's
physical, emotional, and mental states."
Carol Welch

CHAPTER 18

MOVE IT

While hosting a Hollywood awards show several years ago, Steve Martin made the following joke after a well-toned, muscular movie star left the stage. He said,"I would do anything to look like that," then he paused, "except eat right and exercise."

The crowd roared with laughter, and as a viewer I chuckled thinking how his joke pointed out the simplicity of the solution for looking and feeling good.

I'm the first to admit that I regularly fall off the fitness bandwagon. (It's usually at the intersection of a burger place and an ice cream parlor.) I have a gym membership that rarely gets used, and I exert a lot of mental energy thinking about exercising instead of lacing up my shoes and going for a walk.

I no longer have hopes of flat abs and killer thighs. My pursuit of perfection got left behind long ago. However, I know that if I want to stay healthy and vital for many years to come, I have to do some form of activity most days of the week. It's not about having a perfect body (not gonna happen), but about living a better life.

Science shows that regular exercise, including brisk walks, directly increases happiness 12 percent and makes a dramatic contribution to improving self-image. So, if you're like me, and you've been lounging by the pool more than you've been swimming in it, take a look at how you can incorporate some more movement into your daily life. I know I'm going to!

Little Idea

How about sponsoring your own Biggest Loser contest with a group of friends or co-workers. Excercising and eating right with support from others could prove to be just the right combination to help you shed those pounds that just keep hanging around.

"The problem with communication ...
is the illusion that it has been accomplished."
George Bernard Shaw

CHAPTER 19

BECAUSE I SAID SO

Chalk up "Because I said so" to that famous list of phrases that you can only fully understand, appreciate, and utilize once you spend much of your time around inquisitive youngsters. Often in the chaos of everyday living, I find this phrase much simpler to use than a lengthy explanation – especially when I'm not able or willing to share the origin of my decision making process.

However, I might be changing my tune (or at least my verbiage) after reading about an interesting study done by social psychologist Ellen Langer. She found that including your listener in the "why" of a decision increases their cooperation rate from 60 to 94 percent.

That's a whopping 34% increase in a positive response from your listener just by taking another minute to follow the "because" with some real information. I'm not saying this is going to magically work on children, but it might help, and the technique can definitely spill over into other areas of your life – professional and personal. It seems that people will be much more understanding if you let them in on the real "because" of your actions.

So the next time someone asks you "Why?" or you see that "Why are you doing that?" look in their eyes, take a minute to explain yourself. It will be worth it!

Little Idea

Since "because I said so" is one of those classic mommisms, take a little time to reflect on all of the things that you love about your parents. You might get some ideas on what you want to incorporate more of into your own life . . . your Dad's kindness to his neighbors or your Mom's ability to gift wrap the best packages. Sometimes we only focus on the negatives about those who raised us instead of exploring and finding the good stuff. Whether you're still blessed with them here on earth, or they're smiling down from up above, you'll feel a greater connection by reflecting on the good stuff.

"Fashions fade, but style is eternal."
Yves Saint-Laurent

CHAPTER 20

THAT'S SO YOU!

I recently overheard a conversation between two friends at a store in the mall. One shopper picked up a top and said to the other, "This is so YOU!" The other shopper squealed, "I LOVE this," took the top, tried it on, and bought it on the spot. I have to admit that I wondered what my friends would pick out for me besides pajamas and loungewear! Instead of being a slave to fashion, all too often I'm a slave to comfort.

Style is a skill I've been developing for quite a long time, and let's just say I've missed the train a few times. I'm addicted to hoodies and yoga pants, but lately, I see the value in having my wardrobe grow up with me. And yes, unlike some other women my age (and older) I've sworn off the juniors department!

Part of the fun of developing a wardrobe and a personal style is finding clothes that make you feel more like YOU. I view it as a game. Finding a perfect dress, top, or accessory that you LOVE is worth the search. And style isn't about money. I've seen a friend change a whole outfit just by putting on a great pair of earrings that are so her.

The first step is being willing to spend as much on yourself as you do on others in your house. (I'm no stranger to paying more for an outfit for my daughter than I would for an outfit for myself.) Picking up little things that you love and not feeling guilty, is a great way to start having a closet full of things that bring you joy.

Imagine how easy it will be to get dressed in the morning once your closet is full of things that are so YOU! When you look good, you feel good, and when you feel good, you can accomplish anything. So happy hunting!

Little Idea

Take a ruthless look at your closet. Are you holding on to any looks that just aren't you anymore? Imagine what it would feel like to let it go. A great resource for the process is Gail Blanke's book **Throw Out Fifty Things**. *Check it out for inspiration to get you moving toward the closet and life of your dreams.*

"When you are grateful, fear disappears and abundance appears."
Anthony Robbins

CHAPTER 21
TAKE A NUMBER

Things have been a little out of focus for me lately. No, I don't need new glasses. I'm talking about my inability to stay engaged in one task at a time. Rarely, do I start and finish a task all at once. (In fact, my phone just rang; I had a 27-minute conversation, and now I'm back.) As a person living on this planet, I'm sure you've also realized that life is inherently full of distractions.

This isn't a new concept for women. Back in 1955 writer Anne Morrow Lindbergh shared the same sentiment in her classic non-fiction book, A Gift From the Sea, "Distraction is, always has been, and probably always will be an inherent part of woman's life."

So what's a girl to do? Stress about it? Nah – too easy. How about this idea?

Feel flattered.

That's right. Hang up the "poor me" attitude and feel flattered that you can't get through a task without the phone ringing, a child asking for something, a neighbor knocking, or the boss stopping by your desk.

All of these are signs that you're vital to the people around you. Instead of feeling frustrated by having to spread your attention around, accept that distractions are a natural part of being so important to so many people.

So give yourself a pat on the back, a few uninterrupted minutes each day to take a breath, and if you have to, permission to say, "Take a Number!" with a big smile on your face.

Little Idea

So many times we make a list of all of the things yet to be done. Our TO DO lists can overwhelm us at times. What if you make a DID list? List all of the things you have done for the past 7 days. You'll be amazed at how much you've accomplished without giving yourself enough credit.

"I can live for two months on a good compliment."
Mark Twain

CHAPTER 22

THE 2 WORD WONDER

Ever have one of those exceptional days where things (including body parts) stay in their proper place -- your hair, your make-up, what you're wearing all just work? You leave the house feeling positive and exuding some "feel good" energy.

You run into a friend or a co-worker who picks up on the vibe and says, "You look great today." Now comes your big chance to respond. Would you say:

a) "Really? I only paid $9.99 for this shirt."
b) "I should. I spent over an hour getting ready."
c) "Oh, no I don't. You're just being nice."
d) "Puh-lease. I need to lose 10 pounds."
e) None of the Above

Ok, so you could see the "none of the above" answer coming from a mile away. And you probably already know the correct answer. How about a simple and sincere. . .

Thank You.

Doesn't seem too hard does it? But it can be. I admit in the past I've used all of the above at one time or another when on the receiving end of a compliment. But really, Thank You is much easier and has a bonus - it makes the giver feel good too.

In Mary Mitchell's essay on "How To Give and Receive a Compliment" in *The Experts Guide to 100 Things Everyone Should Know How to Do* she says: "Never dispute, disparage, or diminish a compliment. To do so is to insult the giver by questioning his or her judgment, standards, taste, or —worst- sincerity. Much better to smile, savor the moment – and watch for the next chance to offer that great feeling to others."

So now you have a great excuse to enjoy the next compliment you receive. Not only will you feel great, but you'll make the giver feel good too. So just smile big and say those two little words . . . Thank You.

Little Idea

Have you ever thought about writing a note of thanks (via snail or e-mail) to someone you don't know thanking them for something. Whether it's great service, a great article in a magazine, or a favorite song, expressing your thanks makes you and the creator feel extra special.

"Nobody grows old merely by living a number of years.
We grow old by deserting our ideals. Years may wrinkle the skin,
but to give up enthusiasm wrinkles the soul."
Samuel Ullman

CHAPTER 23

TRIPLE DIGIT THINKING

In the midst of your daily chaos, have you ever thought of living to be 100? According to the Census Bureau, there are currently 80,000 people aged 100 or older in the United States. By 2040 there will be over 7 times that many centenarians – about 580,000. So chances are increasing that you'll be a triple digit diva (or dude).

So what can you do today that will help you enter your 100's with vitality and peace of mind? Besides the usual – eating healthy and getting daily physical activity – you can practice being a forward thinker who is open to new experiences.

A survey of 100 American centenarians done by Evercare, a company that coordinates care for senior health, showed that many 100+ year olds are plugged into pop culture. Over a third have watched reality television; over a fourth have watched MTV or music videos, and over six percent have been on the Internet or listened to an iPod. Here's to Groovin' Grandparents!

Looks like if you haven't learned to text, work the

DVR, or explored Facebook, now's your chance. Staying up on the trends and being a part of what's current keeps your mind active and engaged. Maybe it's time to start hanging around with your kids. Ask them to teach YOU a thing or two!

Little Idea

We all know that time can fly unless we set some clear goals. Think about the possibility of experiencing something new every six months. It could be a class you take, a skill you learn, or a trip you plan. Whatever it is, do it intentionally and keep track of it. When you look back, you'll be able to see how keeping things fresh helped you to feel like a kid again.

"Joy is the feeling of grinning inside."
Melba Colgrove

CHAPTER 24

SIMPLE JOYS

Admit it. You have a guilty pleasure. Whether it's a tv show, celebrity gossip, or a trashy beach read, guilty pleasures are mindless, easy and, most of all, bring some effortless enjoyment when we need it. Let's just call them instant mood boosters.

Since I can't spend all my days indulging in my guilty pleasures (like Stayin' Alive, the bad 80's movie starring John Travolta), I've learned to recognize other simple things that make me feel good on a daily basis – a.k.a. a simple joy. What's unique is that these aren't typical objects or occurrences that make people feel good in general. Rather, they are something quirky that is unique to you.

Let me give you an example. Freshly sharpened pencils lead my list of simple joys. For some reason they make me feel happy, productive, and like anything is possible. Weird, right? Not to me.

When you become aware of the small things that bring you joy (like the first Diet Coke in the morning), you train yourself to FEEL GOOD daily.

So what's your simple joy?

Little Idea

Here are a list of a dozen simple joys to inspire you.

1. Playing with the dog.

2. Listening to your ipod with headphones and a great groovy song.

3. Filling your candy jar with your favorite childhood candy and then sharing it with others.

4. Calling your best friend and not talking about the kids or work.

5. Placing a picture of your favorite vacation spot on your nightstand.

6. Having a fresh bowl of fruit on your kitchen table.

7. Buying new dish towels and tossing some of the old ones.

8. Taking a nap for no reason at all.

9. Buying a big pack of Sharpies and a blank notebook.

10. Changing your voicemail message to something that will make others smile.

11. Going out to lunch with a friend.

12. Taking a walk in the rain with a big umbrella.

"The time you enjoy wasting is not wasted time."
Bertrand Russell

CHAPTER 25

MOVIE ANYONE?

Lately, the only time I sit through an entire movie is on an airplane. At home, other things seem too important to indulge in the luxury of marking out an afternoon or evening to watch a favorite flick. When I have free time, I figure that de-cluttering the pantry (which probably still has sweetened condensed milk from the nineties) or doing laundry (aka "The never ending abyss") trump my leisure pursuits.

My hope is that if I stay on top of all these things, life will be easier, more carefree, and happier in general. The only problem? Once I get finished there's always a new task nipping at my heels. And I haven't even mentioned the albatross that I call my garage. So instead of getting an energy boost from my hard work, I feel drained just thinking about the endless list of to do's.

After taking a recent airplane trip where I was able to watch an entire movie, I realized that maybe I have it all backwards. Sometimes what seems like a waste of time is the perfect energy infusion. After watching one of my favorites,

Somethings Gotta Give, I realized what movies help me do --
enlarge my vision of myself. Sometimes we get stuck in our own
world believing that we have to get it all done before we can have
fun. Movies help us engage our imaginations and to see life from
a new perspective.

After watching my movie, I was motivated to finish
some tasks and my creative juices were flowing. I had the energy
to give to some domestic tasks as well as some creative tasks.

I think we all can agree, there will always be one more
thing to do. So consider wasting some time this week and watch
a movie, you just might get a new perspective and some instant
energy.

Little Idea

*Ask the people in your family what their favorite movie is.
Assemble a list of favorites, type it up and make it look good, and
distribute it at the next holiday gathering. It will be fun to see
everyone's choices, and it will provide some good suggestions
for viewing.*

"There are two primary choices in life; to accept conditions as they exist, or accept the responsibility for changing them."
Denis Waitley

CHAPTER 26

THE NAVIGATOR

I'm terrible at reading maps. Just ask my husband. For years I tried to play the part of the navigator on long car trips. It was kind of like Miley Cyrus playing the next Meryl Streep role. Just wasn't happenin'.

However, I did nail the scene where I eloquently and evocatively gave my husband a GPS navigator for Christmas. Turn by turn directions saved our marriage. Ok, so I'm still being a little dramatic, but it has been nice to have someone else doing the navigating.

That got me thinking about how tempting it would be to have a device that could help navigate life. In that syrupy synthesized voice, guidance would be plentiful: "Eat Cheerios for breakfast; Wear ruffled shirt; Call Best Friend; Be nicer to kids; Stop and smell the roses." You get the picture.

It sounds nice at first, but if such a device existed, I'd probably stomp it into a million pieces by the end of the first hour. It's much more exciting to think about consciously being the navigator of your own life each day.

In case you've forgotten (which I seem to do regularly), we all get to individually choose how we navigate our worlds. We can navigate toward Same Ole, Same Ole Street or someplace more exciting like Spontaneity Way or Awe Avenue. It's all about the way we behave each day.

The little choices that you make (how you dress, what you have for lunch, how you react to your kids, who you keep in touch with) are the small turns on the larger road map of life. Each choice you make can put you on a path you enjoy or one that feels as long as those road trips where somebody's "gotta go, gotta go, gotta go, right now" and the next rest stop isn't for miles.

Safe Travels!

Little Idea

Think about life as a roadside buffet. There are so many options and opportunities. Make a list of the things you would like to put on your plate. Are you navigating toward achieving those things or are you off course?

"Kindness is loving people more than they deserve."
Joseph Joubert

CHAPTER 27

THAT LADY

Have you ever been behind the lady at the grocery who takes a hundred and thirty-one dollars and seventy-five cents worth of bread, peanut butter, laundry detergent, and every other item known to a grocery list (including pre-made caramel apples) through the self-checkout? As if this isn't annoying enough, her cell phone rings while she's scanning her items and she ANSWERS it! Meanwhile, the seemingly kind voice that lives in the scanner keeps repeating, "Please place the last item in the bag," over and over and over again while the oblivious lady continues her conversation.

Sounds like a sitcom scene, doesn't it? I'd be more apt to belly laugh if it wasn't a true story. However, I wasn't the one fuming behind said lady; I WAS "that lady". The one I've complained about countless times.

Yep, I admit it. I bought my caramel apples loaded up my eight bags of groceries and made a beeline for the car before anyone could throw me another dirty look. Circumstances dictated that I find the quickest checkout route, and with every manned aisle 3 or 4 deep I decided to go self-checkout. The phone call? It was my daughter who was waiting for me to pick her up after a function at school that night. I didn't want her to be worried.

So why do I feel the need to confess? Because sometimes in our day-to-day routines people do things that annoy us more than elevator music. The easy thing is to get aggravated, take it personally, and complain about it.

Now, I try to see the humor in the situation and think about the very real possibility that one day I'll be "that annoying lady" again. I'll be saving my dirty looks for more important things, like my children.

Little Idea
We all spend our fair share of time in the grocery store. Have you ever thought about how to make it a little more enjoyable? Search "Grocery help" on the Internet and you'll find all kinds of pre-made grocery lists and time saving ideas. One of my favorites is to put on your favorite playlist or audiobook and listen to your i-pod as you cruise through the aisles.

"You can become blind by seeing each day as a similar one.
Each day is a different one, each day brings a miracle of its own.
It's just a matter of paying attention to this miracle."
Paulo Coelho

CHAPTER 28

"LOOK!"

Some days I feel as if running my household is like steering a big ship, except I'm blindfolded, exhausted, and anything but Captain material. The word Titanic flashes through my mind, and I can hear Celine Dion singing in the background.

But other days, if I'm lucky, I get a glimpse of how to keep afloat. In the midst of a zillion things to do, my son gave me that glimpse this week and reminded me how simple it is to stay on course.

Immediately after his birthday party this weekend, he began constructing a ramp, for his new Batmobile, out of canned goods, an old board game, and a box. Once he had perfected the ramp and the jump he said, "Mom, come and watch!" Curled up, enjoying my cupcake and ice cream sedation, my first thought was to stay snug in my chair. However, I dragged myself up to watch, and as Batman ramped up and knocked over the Joker, my son's face lit up as he watched me watching what he had done. I realized that as a witness, I had made a good thing even better (and the effort put forth by me was minimal!).

The next few days I started recognizing how much happiness I bring to my kids (and to myself) by just acknowledging what each of them has going on in their lives. A loose tooth – Wow! An "A" on a test – Fantastic! Unlocking the Super Hula Hoop on a Video Game – No Way!

Sometimes it's tough to stop what I'm doing and "Look", but of all the things I can give my kids, attention is the thing they love the most. And, it's super cheap with an endless supply! Now, if I could only get that Celine song out of my head.

Little Idea

My mom encouraged me to create a photo journal of my kids for one summer. Each day I took one snapshot for a month and pasted it into a mini photobook with a caption. Even though it was only 30 days and 30 pictures, I cherish that book for the glimpse back it offers whenever I need it.

What can you document for 30 days that will bring you joy in the future?

"It takes courage to grow up and become who you really are."

~e.e. cummings

CHAPTER 29

THE DUCT TAPE OF LIFE

Here's a simple question:

What holds you together?

Ok, maybe not so simple, but worth a few minutes of thought. I'm not so clever that I thought of this on my own. It's a concept I'm borrowing from the movie *In Her Shoes.* I do most of my best thinking while watching movies, or at least that's how I rationalize spending a couple of hours relaxing in front of the television with some popcorn.

If you haven't seen the movie, it's a chick flick worth watching (even for guys). The sister dramedy based on a book of the same name by Jennifer Weiner has some great scenes. But I digress -- Back to my original question.

So what is it that holds you together?

In other words, what are the things that allow you to keep it together on days when it would be easier to fall apart? They could even be described as the things that define you.

Some of the things that hold me together are my family, great books, fantastic conversation, the beach, swinging on the porch, taking walks with my daughter, and eating homemade pizza (made by my husband). Some people have sports teams that they're fanatical about or a hobby that is their passion.

Knowing what holds me together keeps me grounded in a world that can be unpredictable at times. And if you can't think of anything, it's the perfect time to start paying attention to the things that make you feel at home in your own life.

Little Idea

The only thing that compares to knowing what holds you together is knowing what holds those you love together. Have you ever asked them what allows them to keep it together even in the midst of chaos and uncertainty. If not, here's your chance. Do it today.

"One of the most tragic things I know about human nature is that all of us tend to put off living. We are all dreaming of some magical rose garden over the horizon – instead of enjoying the roses blooming outside our window today." Dale Carnegie

CHAPTER 30

A HEARTY APPETITE

I can eat with the best of them. Sure, I try to limit myself most of the time, but I recently ate my way through a short vacation. In other words, appetite has never been a problem for me. That got me thinking that it would be nice to have a voracious appetite for other (less pleasant) things in life like de-cluttering, organizing photos, or even exercising.

I let myself off the hook knowing I'm not the only one who struggles to keep up with all the "stuff" of life. Not to go all Polly Positive on you, but I decided it's more important to have an appetite for life as it is. I'm all for hoping, wishing and dreaming, but when it comes down to daily happiness much of mine comes from accepting and enjoying what's going on at the moment.

This isn't a free pass to stick with something negative in your life, rather it's a challenge to enjoy your place in the big picture of life right now, as is in all its age related glory.

For example, I'm pretty sure that as much as I wish for it, I'm not going to be an oceanfront barmaid in a palm tree dense locale anytime soon. I think my kids would miss me, or at least miss the carpooling that I provide. I'm also fairly certain that I won't be relishing in the luxury of a clutter free house for oh, the next 10 years or so. In fact, I'm certain when the time comes, I'll miss the various "kid clutter" that brings our house alive these days – even if falling over action figures and Nerf footballs is an occupational hazard of working at home.

It's not always easy to enjoy what you have on your plate, but if you learn to have an appetite for your life as it is right now, you'll start finding ways to make the best of what's right there waiting for you. And that's a good appetite to have.

Little Idea

Many times we get stuck thinking of all of the "if onlys" in our lives. We think "if only I had more time, more money, more connections . . ." then we could enjoy life. If we take a step back and look at our "if onlys" we'll see that they are the very things keeping us stuck. What are your "if onlys"?

"The family is one of nature's masterpieces."
George Santayana

CHAPTER 31

QUIRKY

So the other day I'm driving home from another semi-great (ok, average) meal produced by me with the help of O'Charley's. (I said *produced* not *made*. Big difference.) My son starts clapping to the latest #1 song on Top 20. "Stop clapping," I shout over the noise of the radio. "Why?" he asks. Good question, I think. "I don't know. I just can't stand the sound of clapping in the car," I say. To which my kids crack up at the absurdity of my statement.

Who knows why clapping in the car ranks among one of my top pet peeves. It's just one of those quirks that I'm sure my kids will grow up and discuss with their therapists. But, as we all know, Moms can be and deserve to be quirky now and then.

In fact, people have long exploited family members' oddities, pet peeves, and general behavior for the enjoyment and profit of others. Think *Cosby Show* and *Everybody Loves Raymond.* Can't we all relate to the "realness" of said shows?

I recently read the book *You're Lucky You're Funny*, a non-fiction account of How Life Became a Sitcom by Phil

Rosenthal, the producer of *Everybody Loves Raymond*. In it he describes how much of the material for the show was pulled from his own and cast members' real lives. He says, "But the key was specificity. I didn't know it then, but I learned that this was the universal element. What I stumbled onto was that each of our lives deals in specifics, and we can relate to the specificity in other people's lives."

I think we can all agree that our families have specific things about them that could easily show up in an episode or two of a sitcom. The key is being able to see these things in a humorous light in real life when they aren't on display for millions of people to share in the laughter. Keeping proper perspective on the quirkiness that surrounds you everyday can be freeing and very, very funny.

Little Idea

One of the best stress relievers we can give ourselves is a bit of laughter. Watching old sitcoms, a funny movie, or reading some humor helps to keep things in perspective. Make sure you have a stash of materials that are sure to produce guaranteed belly laughs.

*"Gratitude helps you to grow and expand;
gratitude brings joy and laughter into your life
and into the lives of those around you."*
Eileen Caddy

CHAPTER 32

SET YOUR DIAL

I have the privilege of writing a humor column for a local magazine. One of the top questions I get asked is, "How do you come up with your ideas?" People are usually a bit disappointed when I don't have a magic formula or some sophisticated answer. "I just think of them," I say. But after a little more reflection, I'd like to amend my answer. I say, "Life is filled with all kinds of ideas. It just depends on what you're looking for."

The column has forced me to pay attention to the absurdity of my life. I have to say it's a pretty good job to have when you're forced to find the funny. I've gotten used to setting my dial each day to look for the humor in every day life. Now that I've changed my perspective, I can uncover the seed of humor in most any situation. Things that would have left me deathly embarrassed or utterly furious now have a larger purpose.

I think that we can all "set our dials" and decide what we want to "see" each day: humor, goodness, kindness, fun, happiness, gratitude, love. All of these things are out in the world just waiting for us to pay attention to them. It's not that we don't already know these things exist, we just fail to set our dials each day so that we can consciously look for and witness what we want to see in the world.

So ask yourself, "Have I set my dial today to see what I want to see?" You'll be amazed at the things that show up once you know what you're looking for.

Little Idea

I know we've all heard of this idea, but have you actually tried it? Make a gratitude journal. Jot down several things each morning or evening that you are thankful for. You'll be surprised by how you naturally look for things throughout the day to fill your list.

"For the vast majority of beasts on this planet, stress is about a short-term crisis, after which it's either over with or you're over with."
Robert M. Sapolsky

CHAPTER 33

HIDDEN TALENTS

Not to brag, but over the years I've become a pro at certain day-to-day things. I can make a school lunch in about 90 seconds. I can find missing shoes, books, and electronics in half the time of anyone else in my house. And, I can simultaneously fold laundry, quiz a child, and watch Oprah. Don't be jealous – I'm sure that you have your own hidden talents.

But, I'm also a pro at some not so good stuff – like STRESS. I can worry, have anxiety, and brood with the best of them. If stressing out were an Olympic sport, I just might pull a Michael Phelps. And, my stellar event would be anticipatory stress. I know, I'm whipping out the big terms, but it means exactly what it sounds like. I spend time anticipating things that haven't happened (some would call these imaginary events) and feeling the very real effects of stress in my body. My muscles tense, my stomach churns, and I'm sure my blood pressure climbs up the charts. And if anticipatory stress strikes in the middle of the night, it ratchets up my anxiety by about 110 percent. Things always seem worse in the middle of the night, don't they?

Lately, there have been plenty of things in the news to feed my stress habit. Lucky for me, I've also been studying how consistent stress is terrible for my overall health. Prolonged stress increases risks for slow forming ailments such as heart disease, some types of cancer, immune suppression, and more. Our stress response was intended to kick in to help us survive physical danger, however, we humans have figured out how to constantly engage it by merely imagining events that may or may not happen. The problem is that the stress response becomes more harmful in the long run than many actual stressors (most of which never come to fruition).

So what's the answer? Well, just knowing about the concept of anticipatory stress has helped me to quell my 3 am worries. I can recognize that I'm caught up in a cycle that isn't helping my body or my problem. Sure, thinking ahead about a perceived stressor can help us be prepared, but most of us get carried away thinking about things we can't control or that are unlikely to happen.

When we recognize the anticipatory stress trap, we can be better about avoiding it. That's one talent I'm going to start practicing.

Little Idea
*When you start to stress out the next time, ask yourself which is worse . . . the stressor or **the thoughts** about the stressor?*

"Nobody can go back and start a new beginning,
but anyone can start today and make a new ending."
Maria Robinson

CHAPTER 34

STAGE APPRECIATION

If you ever want to practice maneuver ability without a car, simply drive a cart around Toys R Us like I did recently. Chances are good that you'll have a few fender benders or at the very least experience aisle aggravation, a close relative of it's meaner and profane relative, road rage. I know what you're thinking, and no, I didn't use obscenities on the sacred ground of Geoffrey the Giraffe. But I did experience a level of agitation that I don't recall having on prior trips there.

Ever the self-reflecting questioner (a quality which can drive my husband temporarily insane), I wondered why I was feeling so frustrated. A few Dr. Phil moments later and my self-diagnosis came in as a clear case of parent of tweener blues. With my kids now 10 and 11, the best of my toy store days are behind me. Most presents in my house now come with a charger or in a gift card envelope. The boxes get smaller while the prices get bigger. Gone are the big, colorful Little Tykes creations that I regularly cursed and tried to find space for. I never thought the day would come when I would miss all that plastic in the house.

So what was the end result of my mini self-analysis? After a day of a self-indulgent pity party, I realized the importance of appreciating every stage of life as it comes with all its pros and cons. There is no benefit in pining for days past or worrying about days to come. The time to celebrate is now, even if it's the small things along the way . . . like being able to eat an entire Thanksgiving dinner without having to cut up someone's food or pace the floor with a fussy baby; like being able to relax more while decorating the tree since my kids can now reach higher branches; and like being able to begin to see (for all of you who still have the luxury of rocking babies and the dread of 3am wake up calls) that all of that early hard work of parenting is paying off -- my kids are becoming interesting people. So no matter what the stage, this is your reminder to celebrate the unique opportunities of each phase with all of the blessings (and the few curses) it has to offer.

Little Idea
So many times we concentrate on what we don't have instead of what we do have. I've been inspired by one woman's philosophy to start living each day with enthusiasm. Read Loretta LaRoche's **Life Is Short Wear Your Party Pants** *for an instant pick-me-up.*

"That the birds of worry and care fly over your head, this you cannot change, but that they build nests in your hair, this you can prevent."
Chinese Proverb

CHAPTER 35

FOR THE BIRDS

I've never been a big fan of birds (apologies to the ornithologists). My slight dislike for the winged creatures changed to disdain several years ago at Disney World where I was enjoying a mountainous cone of vanilla soft serve. Mid lick, a seagull buzzed my head, knocked the cone to the ground, and invited a few dozen of his hungry relatives to the feast. My husband delights in retelling this story, especially the part about the look of terror on a bystander's face. "Classic," he says.

So now that you know the backstory, you can appreciate why the following Chinese proverb - that just happens to use birds as an analogy - caught my attention:

That the birds of worry and care fly over your head,
this you cannot change,
but that they build nests in your hair,
this you can prevent.

Ok, so I'm not sure I could have prevented the infamous seagull incident (although I now eat all ice cream inside), but this bit of Oriental thought reminded me that I can choose how I deal with all of the negativity that's swirling around these days. The one thing I can control in the midst of economic chaos, holiday panic, and a general sense of unease is my reaction to it all. The question I'm asking is are you letting the birds of worry build nests in your hair? And just for the record, my answer to that is a big, fat NO! What's yours?

Little Idea
One of the best ways to immediately decrease your worries is to make a list of all of the things that are "flying around your head"these days. When you see all of them on paper, you can decide which ones are worth worrying about and which you can kick out of the orbit above your hair. It's an immediate stress reliever.

"Music washes away from the soul the dust of everyday life."
Berthold Auerbach

CHAPTER 36

INTERRUPTED

When I was 10, I spent hours in my room with my table-top record player – remember the kind that came in a portable case and you had to place the needle on the record for it to start? My album of choice in those days was Michael Jackson's *Thriller*. I spent hours in front of the mirror choreographing dance moves and learning the lyrics. As I look back, it's tempting to think of that time as wasted, but when I'm truthful, I realize that listening to that album (and a bunch of others) made me completely and utterly happy.

I'm sure we could all chronicle our lives in songs ... the one we fast danced to with our girlfriends, the one that consoled us through our first break-up, the one that became an anthem of college independence, the one that we picked for our wedding, the one that we sang to our babies . . . the list goes on and on.

Now that life is so busy, I have to remind myself how important music is in my life. Perusing itunes or spending a half an hour in the CD section of Barnes and Noble (where you can listen to any CD in the store through headphones) might seem like a waste of time, but after doing it recently, I realize that taking time to discover music truly enhances my life. It's been great to unearth some long forgotten songs and discover some new ones. As I once read, "Great music should interrupt your life," and that's just what some songs do for me. Consider how music helps bring you to life!

Little Idea

If you haven't already, check out some of these artists. Finding new music is always a great way to relax, refresh, and renew.

Sam & Ruby
Mat Kearney
Grace Potter
Gavin DeGraw
Ben Taylor
Nikka Costa
Mark Minelli
James Morrison

"There must be a time of day when we, who make plans, forget our plans and act as if we had no plans at all. There must be a time of day when we who have to speak fall very silent."
Thomas Merton

CHAPTER 37

THE PAUSE BUTTON

After going non-stop last week, I rewarded myself on Friday by spending some time with a favorite companion – the DVR. I refuse to feel guilty (which is an accomplishment in itself) about taking a chunk of time to be lazy. I deserved it, and I'm sure that all of you deserve some downtime after facing the daily grind at full-speed. One of the reasons the DVR is one of my favorite inventions of all time is that you can push pause whenever necessary to address whatever situation pops up.

That got me thinking about how important it is to be able to push the pause button on our lives every once in a while. Most people (including me) find this impossible to do on a regular basis. There's always one more thing to finish, to fix, to put away, to fill out, and on and on. I've given up on any kind of semblance to how and when I push the pause button. I don't want "RELAXING" to be one more thing on a never ending To Do List.

Instead, I keep a watchful eye for any opportunity that comes up in the normal course of the week where I can step out of the demanding routine to do something enjoyable to me. Once you get used to stomping out the guilt that comes with slowing down for a minute, it becomes easier and easier to enjoy the free time that you find. We all know that there will be plenty of expected and unexpected things for us to do once we jump back in to the mix, so try to truly enjoy the moments that you get a chance to push pause.

Little Idea

One of the best at learning to push the pause button is Joan Anderson. She has written several bestselling books including **A Weekend to Change Your Life***. This book is a great way to conduct your own mini retreat.*

"I have found that if you love life, it will love you back."
Artur Rubinstein

CHAPTER 38

CAPTURING

I'm willing to bet that the majority of you are the designated family photographer and resident historian. I'm also ready to lay down cold, hard cash that this isn't a position you had to lobby and campaign for. You probably stepped up to the plate because it's one of those "somebody has to do it" kinds of tasks (although I have to note that it's one of the more plush jobs in the category).

Personally, I've held the memory keeper job for over thirteen years now, and I've definitely changed my approach over time. The first years of marriage and motherhood are categorized and cross-referenced in photo boxes. Everything from our first disaster of a Christmas tree to our daughter's first trip to the neighborhood playground are contained in the hundreds of photos organized in chronological order. Recent years are mostly contained as digital images on the computer that I'll get to someday.

Through it all though, one thing hasn't changed, in addition to the photos, which I've become a bit of a slacker on,

I've made sure to keep up with capturing my kids' personalities through the years with small entries in a notebook. The entries remind me of things they have said or done that I don't want to forget. When I look back through this book, I can see the essence of who they are in full swing at each stage.

The trick to capturing in this way is to not let it become too difficult or too much of a chore. A few sentences scribbled every so often at the end of a long day will be one of your favorite possessions in the years to come. And don't put too much pressure on yourself, a few entries a year will be priceless in the future.

Little Idea

Get a notebook where you can jot down some of your favorite memories. Sometimes we get overwhelmed thinking about doing a task, and we just don't do anything. We're paralyzed. This notebook shouldn't be high pressure. Just take a minute every now and then to jot some things down. You won't regret the time invested.

*"Clarity of mind means clarity of passion, too; this is why a great and
clear mind loves ardently and sees distinctly what it loves."*
Blaise Pascal

CHAPTER 39

CLARITY

It happened again the other day. The junk drawer finally stopped
taking deposits. It wouldn't shut. Ok, it shut, but it did that
annoying thing when I tried to open it, and it only half opened
due to a Sharpie lodged between a hidden pair of reading glasses
and a bouncy ball. I scraped my hand through the opening to
clear the way. As I looked down into the randomness, I knew
I had to face reality. Judging by the "new baby" card that I
meant to mail a friend who now had a one year old, I knew I was
looking at almost a year's worth of junk.

The funny thing is it took me about 15 minutes to clean
it out. And after I finished, I felt FANTASTIC. Ok, that's a
smidge dramatic, but between the snow tumbling down outside
and me feeling pent up in the house, it's the little things that
excite me these days.

Why should you care about my junk drawer woes? Well,
it got me thinking about how much mental junk I have stored
away these days. When my mental junk drawer gets overloaded,
I start to feel a little stuck too. I tend to focus on fear and visit

the dreaded land of "what ifs" – a downward spiral of a place if you let yourself fall prey.

So I'm trying to purge the mental junk too. Not as easy as throwing away old restaurant menus and eraserless pencils, but I'm working on it. Being grateful day to day and focusing on ridding the thoughts of fruitless worry are helping me to clear the mental clutter and get unstuck.

Ask yourself how much mental junk you're carrying around. And don't underestimate the clarity inducing power of cleaning out a drawer or two.

Little Idea

A great resource to get some mental clarity is **mythoughtcoach.com**. *The affirmations, meditations, and workouts on this site have helped me to achieve better balance in my life.*

"I get by with a little help from my friends."
John Lennon

CHAPTER 40

BUBBLEGUM FRIENDS

Remember the good old days when finding friends was as easy as offering them a length of Bub's Daddy at the ball fields? I'm thankful to say that I still have some of those friends from the Lindenwald Little League concession stand, but recently I've been thinking about the way new friendships have the power to enrich life, and how hard they can be to find. I'm talking the size of your social network – the people you can depend on and that depend on you when life gets overwhelming.

This doesn't just happen overnight, but if you open yourself up to the possibility of finding a few more close friends, your body and mind will thank you for it. As humans, we're hardwired to be among others, and when we aren't, our bodies send out distress signals that mirror pain. Our stress inducing hormones increase, and we're more likely to have a suppressed immune system.

On the flip side, studies show that as we age, the amount of contact that we have with friends increases our life satisfaction and adds years to our longevity. Participating in groups or activities in which we have a true interest (taking a class, volunteering, going to a hobby based gathering) is one of the easiest ways to connect with others who have similar interests. Friendships take time to grow, but the first step is being open to expanding your inner circle and taking the lead. Life gets better when you share it (and your bubblegum).

Little Idea

Take the lead when it comes to making a new friend. Ask a co-worker, another mom, or someone that you've met in an organization but haven't had the chance to get to know out for a quick coffee or juice break. You'll know right away whether or not you've found someone to create a friendship with. If not, no big deal. Just keep searching! But if you do hit it off, you'll be doing yourself and them a favor both mentally and physically.

*"In any moment of decision the best thing you can do is the right
thing, the next best thing is the wrong thing,
and the worst thing you can do is nothing."*
Theodore Roosevelt

CHAPTER 41

BANANA BOAT MOMENTS

I'm sure you've probably noticed, but the amount of choices for just about anything is overwhelming these days. I'm reminded of a time that I spent close to 15 minutes in the sunscreen aisle at Target, choosing and re-choosing among the countless brands, spfs, and scents. All in all, I was afraid I wouldn't choose the right one. What if I got home and I didn't like it? What if I wasted the $7.99? What if it didn't work and the kids turned up burnt? (I never asked, "What if I waste 15 precious minutes of my life debating the benefits of Banana Boat Sport vs. Banana Boat Ultra Defense?")

Obviously, I was having one of those moments where indecision is king, and I'm its loyal servant. I had a clear case of loss of perspective. I mean fretting over SUNSCREEN – surely, there was a better use of my time.

It's easy to let life's little decisions eat up too much time and energy if we aren't careful. We can get stuck in the indecisive mode for all kinds of choices – wallowing around in the options instead of choosing one and compensating later if necessary. A simple tool for living an Extra-Ordinary life is the power to make a decision and move forward. Obviously, we're moving beyond the sunscreen realm, but you'll reap the benefits if you focus on making clear decisions and getting out of the "I don't know. I'm not sure. What if . . . What if . . . What if mode."

As our world grows and expands, so do our options. We just have to be sure to not let all of these choices make our lives more complicated. One of the best feelings in the world is the moment after you have made a decision. Don't rob yourself of the feeling by second guessing.

Little Idea
Check out the creative decision making techniques presented by Edward DeBono. His approach kickstarts the decision making process and helps you to get more done in less time. My favorite title is **Thinkertoys**, *but his book* **Serious Creativity** *discusses his decision making tools.*

"The energy of the mind is the essence of life."
Aristotle

CHAPTER 42

SALT SHAKER

Ever wonder why you can push through jet lag, a time difference, and little sleep in Vegas, but in day to day life you can't seem to make it to 3:00 in the afternoon without wanting to curl up for a quick bit of shut eye? Or why when you go out to dinner with friends, the thought of being tired doesn't even cross your mind, but when it's time to clean out the garage you can't stifle the countless yawns?

We all have to do things throughout the day that are less than thrilling whether at home or at work. The key is to be able to sprinkle the day with quick pick me ups and little bits of things you love, so that you get an instant energy boost just when you need it.

Without energy and vitality, we can spiral downward into an endless succession of days that seem like something out of the movie Groundhog Day. Sure it would be great to do something we loved every single minute of the day, but that's not reality. However, you do have a choice. You can squeeze in a few minutes of happiness here and there that will help to keep your energy level and mood high. Think of a salt shaker of happiness that you pick up several times a day, sprinkle a little, and add more energy to your life.

The more you make simple changes to find the EXTRA the more energy you will have to sustain you through the mundane moments we all encounter.

Little Idea

It's great to have a go to list of energy boosters for those days when we're just not feeling up to speed. Here are a dozen of mine:

1. Music - instant attitude adjustment

2. Funny You Tube clips - search bloopers

3. Drive thru for a fountain soda

4. A quick spritz of perfume and make-up refresher

5. A bottle of water

6. Get up and move - even if for a minute

7. Make a did list - the things you've done in the past week

8. Text a friend just to say hey

9. Bring some color into your life - pens, candies, folders

10. 3 Deep breaths . . . 3 times

11. Make a list of 25 things you're grateful for

12. Smile - even if you're the only one in the room

"Energy and persistence alter all things."
Benjamin Franklin

CHAPTER 43

MUSIC TO YOUR EARS

When my daughter asked to take guitar lessons last Fall, I wrote it off as another passing phase. When she was still asking around Christmas, I figured it was time to take her seriously. So under the tree was a guitar that I realized had a 50/50 chance of being the next great clothes hanger by the same time next year. I had visions of my poor flute that got cast aside after a frustrating few weeks in the fourth grade.

I'm happy to say that this week, after two months of lessons, we have music! What for weeks were random notes are now parts of "Stand By Me" and "Ghostriders." She has already far surpassed my musical ability (not to mention my patience). Rarely, do I get such an up close and personal reminder of the power of persistence and the invigorating confidence that comes from learning something new. My daughter lights up when she's playing for us.

Sometimes in our instant world, I forget that doing anything well requires showing up and putting in the time -- that includes relationships with ourselves and others, new skills we want to learn, and the qualities in ourselves that we want to develop. Putting our noses down and pressing forward isn't easy in a new endeavor, but if we can just keep doing the work, the payoff is huge, and regardless of what you're doing, the end result will be music to your ears.

Little Idea

Have you ever thought of taking a class, but you don't want to schedule the time away from home? The options for on-line classes are limitless. Two sites I have used with success are Gotham Writers Workshop at www.writingclasses.com and Writer's Digest classes at www.writersonlineworkshops.com. Any area of expertise is bound to have some at home learning you can do. Research some things that you've always wanted to learn how to do. And have fun!

"The moments of happiness we enjoy take us by surprise.
It is not that we seize them, but that they seize us."
Ashley Montagu

CHAPTER 44

WHO?

Several years ago I picked my son up at preschool and decided that since we had the whole day to spend together, we might as well go to the local amusement park. He was thrilled and felt like a king since he was going solo. As we entered the park and started walking around, he looked up at me and said, "This is the Mom I never knew!"

Of course, I cracked up, but the moment has stayed with me. Since then, I've often asked myself, "How can I be the person my (fill in the blank -- husband, kids, parents, siblings, friends) never knew?" In other words, what can I do that might be out of the ordinary that will bring a surprise dose of joy to someone else?

Most of us have a tendency to hold back when it comes to being delightful to others. As we grow up, we begin to create a shell around us that is layered with thoughts and limitations of how we are supposed to act. When we break out of that shell occasionally and go above and beyond expectations, something magical happens. We feel a hopefulness about life and those we share it with. And it doesn't require visiting Sponge Bob at a themepark (although this scores big points with the preschool crowd). It can be as simple as leaving a note for someone or baking something for them for no reason at all. I'm sure you're filled with your own great ideas. Now, you just have to put them in action and be the person they never knew!

Little Idea

Sometimes a bit of inspiration is all that is necessary for you to enlarge your vision of yourself and what you can do for others. I get a good dose of inspiration everytime I watch a TED talk. Google TED talks to see what I'm talking about!

*"If you ask what is the single most important key to longevity,
I would have to say it is avoiding worry, stress, and tension.
And if you didn't ask me, I'd still have to say it."*
George Burns

CHAPTER 45

STRESS AND BACKPACKS

So what do overstuffed, smelly, grade schooler's backpacks and stress have in common? Lots, but you have to stick with me for a minute. When speaking at a Moms Group yesterday, I brought along my friend, Mr. Backpack and some canned goods.

Think of the backpack as the place where you store your chronic low-level stress. And think of the stressors as labeled canned goods. The canned goods might be labeled with the following things:

My daughter is struggling in school.
My husband and I are arguing more.
The roof needs repaired.
I need to clean out the pantry.
I have to pay bills with less money.
My boss expects too much of me.
I don't have time to exercise.

Imagine loading these cans into your backpack. Some of the cans are huge, and some are small depending on how much stress each creates in your life. Before you know it, your backpack is full and heavy, and you have to carry it around with you all of the time. Imagine what a drag that can be on your health and your state of mind.

So what's a person to do with all that stuff in the backpack? Well, the first step is to pay attention to what's in there. When you're aware, you can take ACTION to manage the stress you are carrying around. You can get rid of some canned goods completely by checking things off of your to do list. Others will never fully go away, but with some attention, a jumbo sized canned good might be exchanged for a smaller, lighter version.

The second step is to remember to take off your backpack on a regular basis. Being able to shed the extra weight of our problems by practicing stress reducers, helps us to stay positive. Meditation, taking a walk, exercising, listening to music are all great ways to escape from the backpack for a few minutes.

So, how heavy is your backpack?

Little Idea

Take an inventory of your backpack. When you can see what is stressing you, you take the first step in managing that stress. What can you eliminate from the backpack by just getting something finished (that leaky faucet) and what can you manage by changing your own thoughts (under-reacting to that annoying friend)? Lighten your backpack today.

"You see things; and you say 'Why?'
But I dream things that never were; and I say, 'Why not?'"
George Bernard Shaw

CHAPTER 46

TWO MINUTE TANGO TO HAPPINESS

Think back to your high school or college graduation. Do you remember how filled with vision you were? You could imagine yourself doing just about anything.

Fast forward a decade or more. Somewhere along the way we stop imagining the possibilities and start imagining the limitations. We imagine why something won't work instead of why it will; why we can't do something instead of why we can. This is the dreaded Limitation Syndrome. It starts as a "This won't work because . . ." and ends with feeling stuck in an Ordinary life.

So what's the antidote?

Use your imagination for good.

Before we can achieve anything in our lives – whether it's a cleaner car or winning an Oscar – first we have to envision it. We have to see it in our minds. The problem is that we're so busy running around all day and so tired when we finally stop that we don't dedicate any time to imagining the good things that might be.

Even if you spent just two minutes a day imagining what would bring you joy, you will have invested over 12 hours in your vision of joy by the end of one year. And most likely, some of those joy filled imaginings will have actually happened because you focused your attention on them.

Unfortunately, we never seem to have too little time for imagining the limitations, but if we give equal time to the positive possibilities we can bring more joy and happiness into our lives.

Little Idea

Experiment with some new ways to spark your imagination. If you've never read poetry, or you have a negative view of it because of your 11th grade Lit Class, give it a try. A few personal favorites follow:

"Wild Geese" by Mary Oliver
"Is My Soul Asleep?" by Antonio Machado
"Today Like Every Other Day" by Rumi
"Fire" Judy Brown
"Imperfection" Elizabeth Carlson
"Mother to Son" Langston Hughes

"Some people think it's holding on that makes one strong –
Sometimes it's letting go. "
Unknown

CHAPTER 47

LYRIC LESSON

Have you ever been listening to a song that you've heard dozens of times when one of the lyrics just jumps out and seems to smack you up side the head? (In a good way, of course!) I had a smackable experience recently when listening to a Rascal Flatts song. The simple lyric *"Holding on and letting go, she just keeps givin' in"* suddenly made perfect sense to me.

Lately, I've realized that life requires us to do both of these things on a regular basis – holding on and letting go. Funny thing is that we have to do these polar opposites simultaneously to keep our lives fresh and meaningful.

Everything from cleaning out the pantry, to sorting through the kids' toys, to developing relationships with our children requires a constant keeping of the good stuff and a constant pruning of the bad stuff that just isn't working. It's a tough job to know what to keep and what to throw out, but if we really just listen to our gut, 99% of the time we get it right. And is there any better feeling than finally letting go of something that no longer makes sense in our lives? It's liberating, scary, and exhilarating.

Ok, maybe this doesn't apply to old hot dog buns, but it certainly applies to thoughts, routines, and ways of doing things that no longer serve us and our visions for our lives. So you might just ask yourself what's worth holding on to, and what's finally reached a time for letting go?

Little Idea

Time to take out that handy notebook you have shoved in the junk drawer and make a quick list. On one side list half a dozen to a dozen things that are working in your life. Maybe it's family dinner time or socializing with friends. On the other side make a list of things that aren't working. Maybe it's that pile of clutter in the kitchen that keeps mounting or not enough exercise. Once you look at what you want to hold onto and what you want to let go, you'll find ways to naturally incorporate more of what you want and less of what you don't. Your list is your roadmap!

"Listening is a magnetic and strange thing, a creative force.
The friends who listen to us are the ones we move toward.
When we are listened to, it creates us, makes us unfold and expand."
Unknown

CHAPTER 48

UH HUH

When is the last time you thought about the word "uh-huh"? I bet you've said it way more than you've thought about it. And yes, it's an actual word. I looked it up to make sure. It's an interjection that dates all the way back to 1889, and Webster's says it expresses affirmation, agreement, or gratification. In my world, it also expresses, "I stopped listening to you ten minutes ago."

Lately, I've come down with a severe case of the "I'm pretending to listen" uh huhs. Whenever my mind gets overloaded, I realize that my listening skills drop dramatically – kind of like a huge brick from the top of a skyscraper. My kids, my husband, and other family members usually feel the ensuing fallout. Lucky for me (and them), I'm trying to be more aware of my tendency to mindlessly bump the bricks.

A true and inexpensive gift we can give to the people (including the little people) that we live with and love is to really listen to what they are saying. More times than not, I'm guilty of tuning out, formulating my next response, or scrolling through my mind's ever present to do list as someone else is speaking to me. Listening is one of those things we tend to take for granted. We think we're just naturally going to be good at it forever. It really takes continued practice and patience to stay on top of our game. So the next time you say uh huh, make sure you really mean it.

Little Idea

Take one day and decide that you will listen more than you speak. Tune in to what people are saying and don't worry about trying to top their story or prove your point. For just one day give others the gift of listening and see what kind of rewards you reap in return.

"Whenever I feel blue, I start breathing again."
L. Frank Baum

CHAPTER 49

GIMME A BREAK

Do you ever feel like the lazy days of summer are so far gone that you can't even remember the sweet smell of suntan lotion? Around here, our lives go from 0 to 60 in 8 seconds flat. School, homework, work, sports, and the general stuff of life have all of us running around most of our waking hours.

And in that spirit, I'm offering a friendly reminder that I have to force myself to do when things get hectic: TAKE A BREAK.

I can hear the chorus now, "Are you crazy? Who has time to take a break?" And my answer would be, "You do." In fact, you must in order to save time later. When our bodies get too tired from constant running, there's a whole list of negative health effects that you'll eventually have to make time for. In fact, did you know that even one minute of concentrating on your breath and mentally letting go of all the stress works wonders to balance your body.

But *you* have to do it for yourself. No one else can make sure you're taking that much needed time to recharge your batteries. I'm sure you have at least one minute to spare in the mix of the everyday stuff. Sitting at your desk or waiting in the car, you can use those extra minutes to take a mini break. There's no secret formula. Just pause, relax your face and shoulders, and take a few deep breaths. Forget everything that's on your plate if only for a minute.

Remember it's the little things that add up to big changes. Take your break. You deserve it!

Little Idea

Just like anything that we get good at, you have to practice taking mini-breaks. At first, it will feel indulgent and like it's not worth the trouble, but over time you'll discover how just a little bit of time can add up to a big attitude adjustment. Start small and take a conscious break at least once a day for the next week.

"One is free like a hermit crab to change one's shell."
Anne Morrow Lindbergh

CHAPTER 50

EASY LIKE SUNDAY MORNING

So, have you ever watched someone do something really well (raise a family, speak in front of a group, make friends, achieve great business results, sing, you name it) and thought, "Wow, if only it was that easy for me!" This thought is especially pervasive on those days when you're experiencing a touch of the woe is me blues. You know, *the grass is always greener, their jeans are always smaller* kind of days when you walk into your closet and even getting dressed seems difficult. (Have you ever had one of those days where you just want to throw out every piece of clothing and start from scratch? . . . Me too!)

Well, I hate to break up the pity party, but much to my dismay, whenever someone makes something look easy, I've discovered 99.9% of the time a large amount of hard work and determination is lurking somewhere in the background.

People who do things really, really well make them look so easy. That's part of the charm of being exceptional at whatever it is you've put your mind to. The hours of blood, sweat, and tears that have gotten a person to a personal peak usually aren't the topic of discussion, their success outshines all of the hard work.

The bad news that comes with this discovery is that you have to toss the "I could never be like that because he's /she's special" excuse. The good news is if you go for something with gusto and give it enough time, attention, and determination, you have the power to make whatever it is you want to achieve look easy too. And when you do, you'll be kicking that woe is me attitude to the curb with all of your newfound energy.

Little Idea

Take some time today and figure out one thing that you want to be better at. Maybe it's meeting new friends or speaking in front of a group. Or, maybe it's a skill you've always wanted like playing the piano or acoustic guitar. Whatever you decide it is, give yourself some time to explore how you can re-engage with your interest. Maybe it's taking a class or finding an on-line resource. Whatever you decide to focus on will get the attention it needs so that you can improve.

"There is little difference in people, but that little difference
makes a big difference. The little difference is attitude.
The big difference is whether it is positive or negative."
W. Clement Stone

CHAPTER 51

VELCRO OR TEFLON

If you've ever done a fair share of gift wrapping, could you imagine if the scotch tape suddenly lost all of its adhesive? How annoying! Most of the time we want things to stick - good habits, relationships, and even things like scotch tape and name tags.

What I'm wondering today, though, is how to get certain things to be less sticky. That's right, I'm thinking it could be a really good skill to learn how to let some things bounce off of us.

For instance, whenever we hear any feedback about ourselves either formal or informal, (possibly, some unsolicited advice or commentary around the family punch bowl or a passing comment from our boss) we tend to let the negative comments stick to us for days, weeks, or sometimes even years! We become instant Velcro. Even if we've heard dozens of positives, we let that one negative hang on, and on, and on, and on.

We sit with it, we stew, and we wonder what we can do to change that person's mind, to prove to them that we didn't deserve that feedback.

In reality, the best thing we can do is to become like Teflon. We can make it impossible for the comment to stick with the right mental attitude.

We always have a choice when it comes to how we react to the words and actions of others. Most of the time, the best method is to under-react. At least, choose to give the positive feedback you hear just as much, or more power than the negative. It seems like we're quick to shrug off the positive comments. Start noticing them!

And as for the negative, we all know that sometimes a little constructive criticism is warranted, but don't let it overshadow everything. Take what you can from the less than perfect feedback, and then let it go. Take off your Velcro suit. It's sure to bring more joy to your life.

Little Idea

Take a minute to think about a piece of negative feedback that has stuck with you over the years. As a professor, I was evaluated every semester, and I remember one student who went on and on about how easy and over simplified my class was. I held onto this comment for months and months before I challenged it. Could I be absolutely sure this was true? No! And the fact that I had taught hundreds of students and this was the first time someone had given that feedback proved to me it was time to let the comment go. What feedback do you need to let go?

*"There is more hunger for love and appreciation in this world
than for bread."*
Mother Teresa

CHAPTER 52

SHOW SOME APPRECIATION

I bet you've become a queen (or king) of multi-tasking. In fact, as you're reading this last chapter, you've probably still got a ticker tape of To Do's rolling through your mind. You may even be folding that last bit of laundry one handed, waiting for a text back from a friend you're worried about, or in standby mode until you are called upon to quiz your fifth grader for his big science test. In any event, you're probably squeezing in reading time, sandwiching it between all of the obligations and responsibilities of the day.

First, let me applaud you for taking a minute to do something nice for yourself. Can you hear my generous clapping? I even let out a woo hoo for you. (Seriously, pause a minute and listen to my appreciation for you. Take a bow, even if it's only in your mind.) You are amazing at keeping all the moving parts working together, even on days when it would be easier to just let them all fall apart.

How do I know this? Well, dear reader, you and I think alike. If you enjoy taking a break to see how you can make your life a little more extraordinary, then we have something in common. And I'm here to remind you how extraordinary it can be to appreciate YOURSELF. I'm not talking about the usual go to the spa, shop for a few hours, or eat an ice cream sundae kind of self-appreciation (although those don't sound bad, do they?). I'm talking about the simple practice of appreciating yourself in your own mind. Giving yourself your own round of applause. Letting that voice inside your head speak with kindness instead of criticism. This kind of appreciation is cheap, easy, and if you get really good at it, it will change the way you interact with life.

Our thoughts (especially about ourselves) can make or break our days, and if we're not careful, they can make or break each year that goes by. When is the last time you told yourself, *"Job well done."* or *"Wow, I got so much done today."* or *"Hooray for me."*?

I'm sure it hasn't been often enough. So join me in gushing about what a great job you're doing. It'll be weird at first, but the fun thing is after awhile, you'll really believe all of those kind things you say to yourself.

Little Idea
Find the EXTRA in the Ordinary by Living in the Little each and every day. Pay attention to enough small stuff and the big stuff will fall into place.

ABOUT THE AUTHOR

Monica Scalf is the founder of The Playground Group, a creative learning company that develops and delivers workshops, keynotes, retreats, virtual learning, blogs, and books. Monica's mission is to help others *find the extra in the ordinary*, that special something that makes individuals exceptional and organizations stand out among the rest. Her award winning writing focuses on finding the joy, energy and humor in everyday life. She lives with her husband and two children in West Chester, Ohio.

Find Monica at mscalf@theplaygroundgroup.**net**
or at 1-877-404-3327.

Read her blog at www.theordinarymatters.com,
or find online workshops and more at
www.theplaygroundgroup.**net.**

45640224R00071

Made in the USA
Charleston, SC
30 August 2015